TAKE A CLOSER LOOK AT YOUR
Muscles

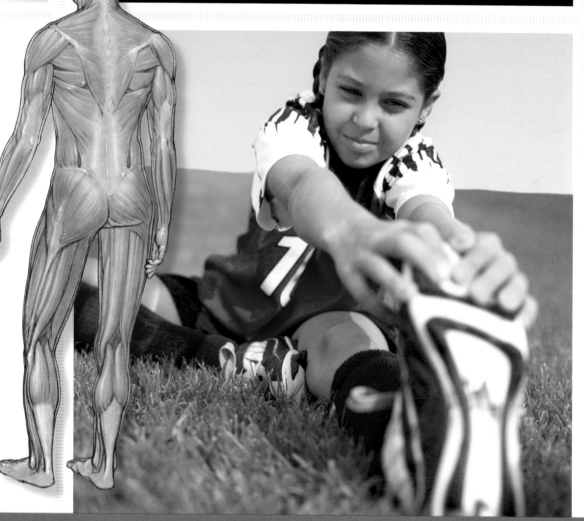

BY JANE P. GARDNER

Published by The Child's World®
1980 Lookout Drive • Mankato, MN 56003-1705
800-599-READ • www.childsworld.com

Acknowledgments
The Child's World®: Mary Berendes, Publishing Director
Red Line Editorial: Editorial direction and production
The Design Lab: Design
Content Consultant: Jeffrey W. Oseid, MD

Photographs ©: Artville, title; Brand X Images, title, 17, 23;
Shutterstock Images, title, 5, 6, 7, 15, 24; Jupiterimages/
Thinkstock, 4, 21; iStockphoto/Thinkstock, 8, 14; Monkey
Business Images/Shutterstock Images, 9; Gunnar Assmy/
Shutterstock Images, 11; Cynthia Farmer/Shutterstock
Images, 13; Photodisc/Thinkstock, 19

Front cover: Artville; Brand X Images; Shutterstock Images

ISBN: 978-1623235512
LCCN: 2013931447

Printed in the United States of America
Mankato, MN
July, 2013
PA02175

About the Author

Jane P. Gardner is a freelance science writer with a master's degree in geology. She worked as a science teacher for several years before becoming a science writer. She has written textbooks, tests, laboratory experiments, and other books on biology, health, environmental science, chemistry, geography, earth science, and math.

Table of Contents

CHAPTER 1

What Are Muscles?

Think of the different ways you have moved today. Did you eat? Run down the stairs? Read the back of a cereal box? Use a pencil? Whisper to your friend? Frown over a hard math problem? If you did any of these things, then you used the muscles in your body.

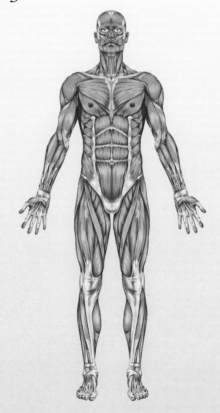

There are many muscles in your body.

Muscles are **tissues**. These tissues work to make your body move. They also help other organs in your body do their jobs. There are more than 600 muscles in your body. Some of these muscles move your bones. Others keep your heart beating or your lungs working. There are muscles in your eyes and in your stomach. Your tongue is also made of different muscles. These muscles help you talk and chew your food. Muscles in your face let you smile, frown, or look surprised.

There are over 50 muscles in your face. That is why you can make such funny faces!

We use muscles to frown and make other silly faces.

Muscles work by tightening and relaxing. Try this activity right now: place your right hand on the upper part of your left arm. Make a tight fist with your left hand. Can you feel how your muscles in the upper arm change? Now relax the left fist. Tighten and relax your fist a few more times. You can feel your muscles in your arm tightening and relaxing. This is how all muscles work.

Your muscles help you move and make different poses.

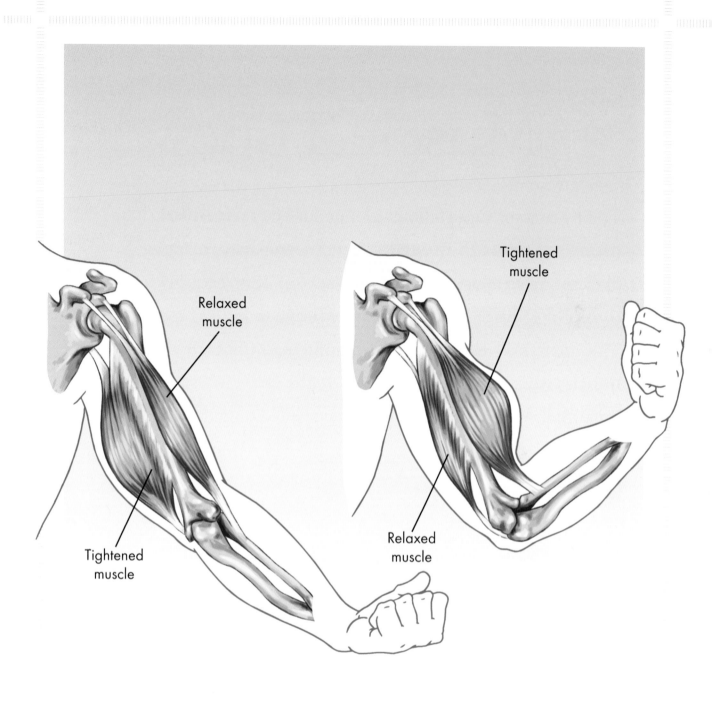

Relaxed
muscle

Tightened
muscle

Tightened
muscle

Relaxed
muscle

Your muscles work by tightening and relaxing.

CHAPTER 2

Muscle Types

There are three types of muscles in your body: **skeletal muscles, smooth muscles**, and the **cardiac muscle**. Skeletal muscles are **voluntary** muscles. This means you can control the muscles. You move your finger to hit a piano key. This uses a skeletal muscle attached to your finger. Skeletal muscles work with the bones to move the body. These muscles are attached to bones by a thin tissue called a tendon.

We use skeletal muscles when we use our fingers.

The muscle that controls your jaw is one of the strongest muscles. It is a skeletal muscle. Chewing food works the muscles in your jaw. Your muscles in your jaw can close your teeth with over 100 pounds (45 kg) of force.

Take a seat! You are now sitting on the biggest muscle in your body – the gluteus maximus.

Muscles in your jaw are very strong.

Smooth muscles are **involuntary** muscles. These are muscles you have no control over. The pupil in your eye changes size when the light in a room changes. You can't stop it because a smooth muscle controls the pupil. Smooth muscles are also found in organs that are hollow. This includes the stomach, small intestine, and bladder.

There are smooth muscles in your esophagus, too. The esophagus is the tube leading from your mouth into your stomach. There are many muscles at work whenever you swallow.

A cardiac muscle is also involuntary. This muscle is only found in the heart. The heart is one big muscle. When the heart muscle tightens, blood is sent out to the rest of the body. When the muscle relaxes, the heart fills with blood again. This muscle beats about 100,000 times each day and you never have to think about it.

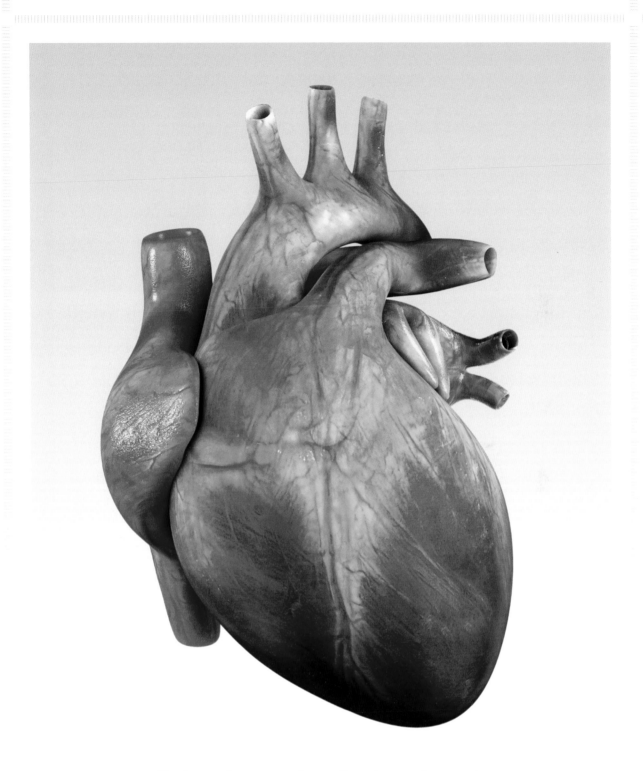

The human heart is made up of one big cardiac muscle.

CHAPTER 3

Problems with Muscles

Chances are your muscles feel sore from time to time. Your arm muscles may be sore after pitching several innings of a baseball game. Or you may feel soreness in your leg muscles after a long hike. Soreness in muscles is natural and usually does not mean something is wrong. Your muscles are simply getting stronger after being exercised.

Muscle **cramps** can hurt. A cramp is a sudden tightening of a muscle. Sometimes the muscle feels hard when it is cramped. Cramps can happen with hard exercise or when a person does not drink enough water. Sometimes cramps happen when there are vitamins missing from someone's diet. Stretching, using ice, and rubbing the muscle can

A painful cramp in your calf is sometimes called a charley horse.

usually help a cramp go away. One way to prevent cramps is to drink plenty of water.

It is normal for muscles to feel sore after exercising for a long time.

Sometimes a muscle becomes too stretched out. This is called a **strain**. A strain can happen suddenly. Lifting a heavy object may cause a strain to the back muscles. Strains can also happen slowly over time. Using the same muscles over and over to swing a tennis racket may lead to strain. The strained muscle may be too sore to use and may swell. Rest is the first step to healing the strained muscle. The muscle may need to be iced. Sometimes wearing a bandage on the strained muscle can help, too.

When a muscle is hurt, resting it and icing it will help make it better.

Your muscles are always working hard.

CHAPTER 4

Keeping Your Muscles Healthy

You use your muscles every day, for almost everything you do. It is important to keep your muscles strong and healthy. One way to do that is by being active. Kids should try to exercise at least 60 minutes each day. Exercise makes muscles stronger. Running, jumping rope, or riding a bike are good things to do. Try out for a team sport. Being part of a team can be fun; you'll make new friends, and it will keep your muscles healthy.

You can break up your exercise into four 15-minute periods of time if you don't have an entire hour. Then you can try four different activities!

Being a part of a sports team will help keep your muscles healthy and moving!

Eating healthy foods can help your muscles. Eating fruits, vegetables, low-fat dairy, and lean meat help you stay at a healthy weight. Being at a healthy weight helps your muscles and bones work well. To help muscles grow, eat meats, beans, and eggs. Bananas and spinach have minerals that help muscles stay strong and healthy.

It is important to keep your muscles free from **injury**. There are things you can do before, during, and after exercise that will keep your muscles healthy. Always be sure to warm up before exercise and cool down afterward. Jog slowly before exercise to warm up your muscles. Cool down after exercise to keep your muscles from getting tight and sore. Cooling down means to slowly stop your exercise.

Eating healthy food is good for your muscles.

Be sure to use your muscles carefully. Practice good habits when lifting heavy objects to prevent strain. Lifting objects by bending your knees can help keep your back muscles healthy.

Always be sure to drink lots of water before, during, and after exercise. Your muscles need water to stay strong. Drinking water, especially when the temperature is warm, will help avoid **dehydration**.

Pay attention to your body. Your muscles will tell you if there is a problem. Don't try to play through the pain during sports or exercise. You risk injury if you don't rest when your body is telling you to. Take good care of your muscles and they will keep you healthy and strong.

Drinking lots of water while you exercise helps your muscles stay strong.

cardiac muscle (KAR-dee-ak MUHSS-uhl) The cardiac muscle is found in the heart. The cardiac muscle beats 100,000 times a day.

cramps (kramps) Cramps are a sudden tightening of a muscle. A muscle can cramp after hard exercise.

dehydration (dee-HYE-dray-shun) Dehydration occurs when more water is lost from the body than is taken in. When it is hot outside, someone may suffer from dehydration.

injury (IN-juh-ree) An injury is damage or harm to the body. An injury can happen if your muscles are not healthy.

involuntary (in-VOL-uhn-ter-ee) Involuntary means to have no control over something. The pupil is an involuntary muscle.

skeletal muscles (SKEL-uh-tal MUHSS-uhls) Skeletal muscles are attached to bones. Skeletal muscles help move the body.

smooth muscles (smooth MUHSS-uhls) Smooth muscles are found in the organs. The stomach is a smooth muscle.

strain (strayn) A strain is stretching or tearing of a muscle or tendon. A muscle strain can happen suddenly.

tissues (TISH-ooz) Tissues are masses of cells with the same function. The muscles in the body are tissues.

voluntary (VOL-uhn-ter-ee) Voluntary means to have control over something. Skeletal muscles are voluntary muscles.

LEARN MORE

BOOKS

Colligan, L. H. *Muscles*. New York: Benchmark Books, 2010.

Simon, Seymour. *Muscles: Our Muscular System*. New York: Harper Collins, 2000.

WEB SITES

Visit our Web site for links about the muscles: **childsworld.com/links**

Note to Parents, Teachers, and Librarians: We routinely verify our Web links to make sure they are safe and active sites. So encourage your readers to check them out!

INDEX